GW01418079

Can't Live With Them,
Can't Live *With* Them

Copyright © Summersdale Publishers Ltd 2000

All rights reserved.

No part of this book may be reproduced by any means, nor transmitted, nor translated into
machine language without the written permission of the publisher.

Summersdale Publishers Ltd
46 West Street
Chichester
West Sussex
PO19 1RP
United Kingdom

www.summersdale.com

ISBN 1 84024 128 4

Printed and bound in Great Britain

Cartoons by Kate Taylor

WOMEN

Can't Live With Them, Can't Live *With* Them

Peter Bighead

SP

SUMMERSDALE

WOMEN

Contents

WOMEN

Jokes

What is a woman's favourite sport?

Jumping to conclusions.

WOMEN

What do you do if the washing machine stops working?

Tell her to get back down to it.

What sport do women
encourage men to do?

Jumping through hoops.

ALWAYS
RIGHT

What should you do if a
woman throws a hand
grenade at you:

*Take the pin out and
throw it back.*

CAN'T LIVE WITH THEM . . .

How many women does it take to make chocolate chip cookies?

Ten. One to mix the dough and nine to peel the Smarties.

What is it when a
man talks dirty
to a woman?

Sexual harassment.

What is it when a
woman talks
dirty to a man?

A very large phone bill.

Why do men fart
more than women?

Because women don't
stop talking long
enough to build up
the pressure.

What's the difference between a terrorist and a woman with PMS?

You can negotiate with a terrorist.

How did scientists work out that there are female hormones in beer?

When they gave a man ten pints of the stuff he talked rubbish and could barely drive a car.

ALWAYS RIGHT

WOMEN

Why does a woman
close her eyes
during sex?

She hates to see a man
having a good time.

ALWAYS
RIGHT

How do you make a
woman's eyes light up?

Shine a torch
in her ear.

ALWAYS
RIGHT

What do you call a woman in a wardrobe?

The winner of last year's hide and seek competition.

ALWAYS RIGHT

What do you call
ten women
standing ear to ear?

A wind tunnel.

ALWAYS
RIGHT

A woman always has the last word in an argument. Anything a man says after that is the beginning of a new argument.

ALWAYS RIGHT

What's six inches long, two inches wide, and drives women wild?

Money.

WOMEN

A beggar hobbled up to
a woman and said,
'I haven't eaten
anything for days.'

The woman replied,
'God, I wish I had your
will power.'

What is the difference between a woman and a battery?

A battery has a positive side.

Home Truths

WOMEN

When women go on a night out, they will spend more time chatting in the ladies' toilets than socialising by the bar.

ALWAYS RIGHT

WOMEN

Why can't women leave
the toilet seat *up*?

ALWAYS
RIGHT

WOMEN CAN'T LIVE WITH THEM . . .

ALWAYS RIGHT

God made man before he made woman because he thought he should create the solution before the problem.

WOMEN

Women complain that
they are miserable – then
they watch a film about a
woman who is terminally
ill and then dies, leaving
behind a husband and
twin daughters – and
thrive on it.

ALWAYS
RIGHT

WOMEN

ALWAYS RIGHT

Women are vain. Not only will they check their appearance in the mirror, they will also check it in shop windows, spoons (or any cutlery available to them), or on their computer screen.

32

Women are just like computers: they crash just when you're starting to enjoy yourself, and they need constant attention to keep them going.

Beware any woman with a father. She will run to him at the first sniff of boyfriend trouble – and he will do his level best to get rid of the offending article – using any method he sees fit.

ALWAYS RIGHT

35

Women love a bargain. And they will always compensate by buying something else equal to the amount they have 'saved'.

WOMEN

Women love to cry –
but won't do it alone
unless they know a man
can hear them.

ALWAYS RIGHT

A woman can't *not* answer the phone, no matter what she is doing.

Women are never wrong. Apologising is a man's responsibility. But remember: it was Eve who gave Adam the apple.

CAN'T LIVE *WITH* THEM . . . WOMEN

ALWAYS RIGHT

A woman will drive miles out of her way because she doesn't want to risk getting lost by using the short cut.

CAN'T LIVE *WITH* THEM . . . WOMEN

What type of car do you drive?

A red one.

ALWAYS RIGHT

There is no point in answering a woman truthfully if she asks you if she looks OK when she doesn't – she does NOT want an honest answer.

44

ALWAYS RIGHT

Women want equal rights – but they're not so happy about the idea of taking the rubbish out, or carrying their own bags.

WOMEN

Women cannot use a
map unless they turn it
around so that it
corresponds to the way
they are headed.

ALWAYS RIGHT

A man will pay half-price for an item that he needs.

A woman will pay double for an item that she doesn't need.

A woman is overweight?
Don't ever argue with
her about it.

A woman is overweight?
Don't ever agree with
her about it.

Men seek entertainment that allows them to escape reality. Women seek entertainment that reminds them of how horrible things *could* be.

Marrying a Woman

Married men should forget their past mistakes. They will be reminded of them often enough.

WOMEN CAN'T LIVE WITH THEM . . .

A philosophical question to think about: if a man speaks in the woods and his wife is not there to hear him, is he still doing wrong?

Men who have pierced body parts are better prepared for matrimony. They have experienced pain and bought jewellery.

ALWAYS RIGHT

Before a man marries
a woman she is sweet,
charming, kind
and generous.

It's all downhill
from there.

CAN'T LIVE *WITH* THEM . . . WOMEN

BEFORE

AFTER

To have more than one husband is bigamy; to have more than one wife is absolute insanity.

Never marry a woman for her money; in the long run a loan shark demands less interest.

WOMEN CAN'T LIVE WITH THEM . . .

A man never worries
about the future
– until he gets a wife.

WOMEN

Losing a wife
can be difficult.

In some cases,
almost impossible.

ALWAYS
RIGHT

WOMEN

Single men die earlier than married men.

Married men are nagged too much to find the time.

There are only two times when a man doesn't understand a woman: before marriage and after marriage.

All wives are the same,
they just have
different faces so you
can tell them apart.

ALWAYS
RIGHT

I married Miss Right. I didn't know her middle name was Always.

Bigamy is having one
wife too many.

Some say monogamy is
just the same.

Do you know the
punishment for bigamy?

Two mothers-in-law.

When she says . . .

WOMEN

When she says . . .
You make the decision.

She means . . .
I've given you enough
pointers, you should
agree with me if you
know what's good
for you.

ALWAYS
RIGHT

WOMEN CAN'T LIVE WITH THEM . . .

When she says . . .
We need to talk.

She means . . .
You're in trouble.

When she says . . .
Do what you want.

She means . . .
You'll pay for it.

ALWAYS RIGHT

72

WOMEN

When she says . . .
No, do go ahead.

She means . . .
But I really don't
want you to.

ALWAYS
RIGHT

WOMEN

When she says . . .
I'm fine.

She means . . .
If you can't see that
I'm not fine you need
your head testing.

ALWAYS RIGHT

WOMEN CAN'T LIVE WITH THEM . . .

When she says . . .
I'm not over-reacting!

She means . . .
I have my period.

WOMEN CAN'T LIVE WITH THEM . . .

When she says . . .
You're very
attentive tonight.

She means . . .
Give it a rest,
won't you?

WOMEN

When she says . . .
Turn off the lights,
it's more romantic
that way.

She means . . .
I don't want you to see
my flabby thighs.

ALWAYS
RIGHT

WOMEN CAN'T LIVE WITH THEM . . .

When she says . . .
Are you asleep?

She means . . .
I'm bored.

WOMEN CAN'T LIVE WITH THEM . . .

When she says . . .
Do you love me?

She means . . .
I'm feeling fat today.

WOMEN

When she says . . .
I hate this kitchen!

She also means . . .
I'm feeling fat today.

ALWAYS
RIGHT

WOMEN CAN'T LIVE WITH THEM . . .

When she says . . .
I'll be ready in a minute.

She means . . .
. . . or fifty.

When she says . . .
I'm not shouting!

She means . . .
The reason I'm
shouting, you moron,
is because this is
important.

WOMEN

When she says . . .
My life is too
complicated.

She means . . .
You can't stay the night
because one of my
other five boyfriends
might turn up.

ALWAYS
RIGHT

WOMEN

ALWAYS RIGHT

When she says . . .
It's not you, it's me.

She means . . .
It's not me, it's you.

Ten Things You'll Never Hear a Woman Say...

ALWAYS RIGHT

WOMEN CAN'T LIVE WITH THEM . . .

1) Oh! She's wearing the same outfit as me! I must go and chat to her. I think it looks better on her, don't you?

2) Let's not bother to
   go to that sale,
   I don't need *more*
   clothes anyway.

WOMEN

4) I can't accept this
ring. The diamond is
just too big.
You must take it back.

ALWAYS RIGHT

5) I'm tired of being 'just friends'. Let's have a 'just physical' relationship.

6) Don't let's stop to ask for directions. I think I know a good short cut anyway.

ALWAYS RIGHT

7) I'm worried that my bum looks too small in this.

WOMEN

8) Let's leave the light on shall we? I like it when you look at my body.

ALWAYS RIGHT

ALWAYS RIGHT

9) I don't like chocolate, so go ahead and finish your dessert, you ordered it for yourself anyway.

10) I can't expect you to buy me a dress for *that* much money – come on, we're leaving the shop.

ALWAYS RIGHT

Seminars
For Women

How to Overcome the Audacious Assumption that You are Never Wrong.

WOMEN

How Not to be Unbearably Self-Righteous When You are Right.

ALWAYS RIGHT

How to Wait for
Another Person to Stop
Speaking Before You
Start Talking.

ALWAYS
RIGHT

How Not to Ask for the Truth When What You Want is Agreement.

Independent Thought:
Your Girlfriends Do Not
Have the Answer.

ALWAYS RIGHT

WOMEN

Sex: More Than Just Lying There.

ALWAYS RIGHT

How to Avoid Walking
in Front of the TV.

WOMEN

Soap Operas:
They are Not Real.

ALWAYS RIGHT

Quotations About Women

I heard a man say that
brigands demand your
money or your life,
whereas women
require both.
Samuel Butler

ALWAYS
RIGHT

WOMEN CAN'T LIVE WITH THEM . . .

The only really happy folk are married women and single men.
Henry Louis Mencken

ALWAYS RIGHT

WOMEN

Women of genius commonly have masculine faces, figures and manners. In transplanting brains to an alien soil God leaves a little of the original earth clinging to the roots.
Ambrose Bierce

ALWAYS RIGHT

Only two things are necessary to keep one's wife happy. One is to let her think she is having her own way, and the other is to let her have it.
Lyndon B. Johnson

WOMEN

Most women have no
characters at all.
Alexander Pope

A woman is . . .

something that gets
mad when you try to
define it.
Piet Grijs

A woman is . . .

the second most important item in a bedroom.
Paul Hogan

WOMEN CAN'T LIVE WITH THEM . . .

A woman is . . .

the eternal question,
and man is the
answer to it.
Sidney Tremayne

Women!
Can't
Live With
Them ...

ALWAYS
RIGHT

If a man doesn't agree with everything a woman says, he is difficult.

If a man agrees with everything a woman says, he is a pushover.

If a man is well-dressed, he's a creep.

If not, he never makes an effort.

ALWAYS RIGHT

If a woman makes a decision without consulting a man, she is liberated.

If a man makes a decision without consulting a woman, he is a selfish pig.

WOMEN

If a man kisses a
woman, he is not
a gentleman.

If he doesn't, he
is not a man.

If a woman has a boring, low-paid job, it is exploitation.

If a man has a boring, low-paid job, he should get off his fat behind and find something better.

ALWAYS RIGHT

WOMEN

If a man tries to keep
himself in shape,
he is vain.

If he doesn't,
he is a slob.

ALWAYS
RIGHT

**For the latest humour books
from Summersdale, check out**

www.summersdale.com